AF575348

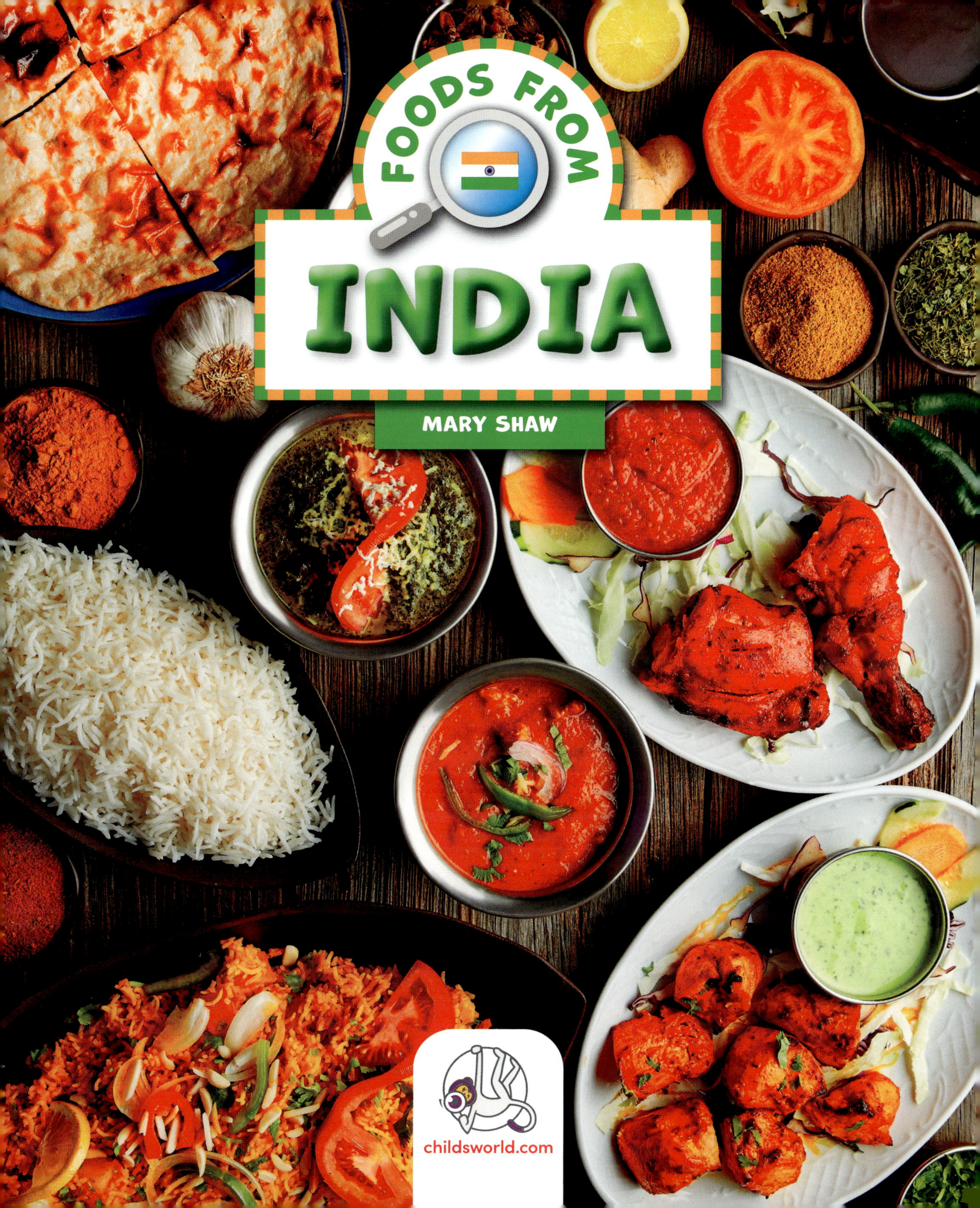
FOODS FROM
INDIA
MARY SHAW
childsworld.com

Published by The Child's World®
800-599-READ • www.childsworld.com

Photography Credits
Photographs ©: Shutterstock Images, cover (background), 1 (background), 3 (background), 5 (globe), 12–13, 17; T. Lesia/Shutterstock Images, cover (flag), 1 (flag), 3 (flag), 4 (flag); Boyko Pictures/Shutterstock Images, 4 (landmarks), back cover; Peter Hermes Furian/Shutterstock Images, 5 (country); Prisca Laguna/Shutterstock Images, 7; iStockphoto, 8–9, 18–19; Tatiana Volgutova/Shutterstock Images, 11; Neeraz Chaturvedi/Shutterstock Images, 14; Ika Rahma H./Shutterstock Images, 20; Candice Bell/Shutterstock Images, 22

ISBN Information
9781503885295 (Reinforced Library Binding)
9781503885660 (Portable Document Format)
9781503886308 (Online Multi-user eBook)
9781503886940 (Electronic Publication)

LCCN 2023937462

Printed in the United States of America

Mary Shaw writes, edits, and designs children's books. She lives in Minnesota with her partner and their two cats. Shaw enjoys cooking and using the ingredients she grows in her garden. She would like to learn how to make mint chutney!

TABLE OF CONTENTS

INDIA

India is a country in southern Asia. It shares land borders with six countries. The island country of Sri Lanka lies to the southeast. India is also bordered by water.

India has many different natural features. The Himalayas are in the north. The climate near this mountain range is cold and windy. Northwestern India has deserts. The country mostly has **tropical** weather. Summers are hot and humid.

There are many **cuisines** and flavors throughout India. Rice is a **staple** in many meals. India has the highest percentage of vegetarians in the world. Hinduism is a religion with many followers in India.

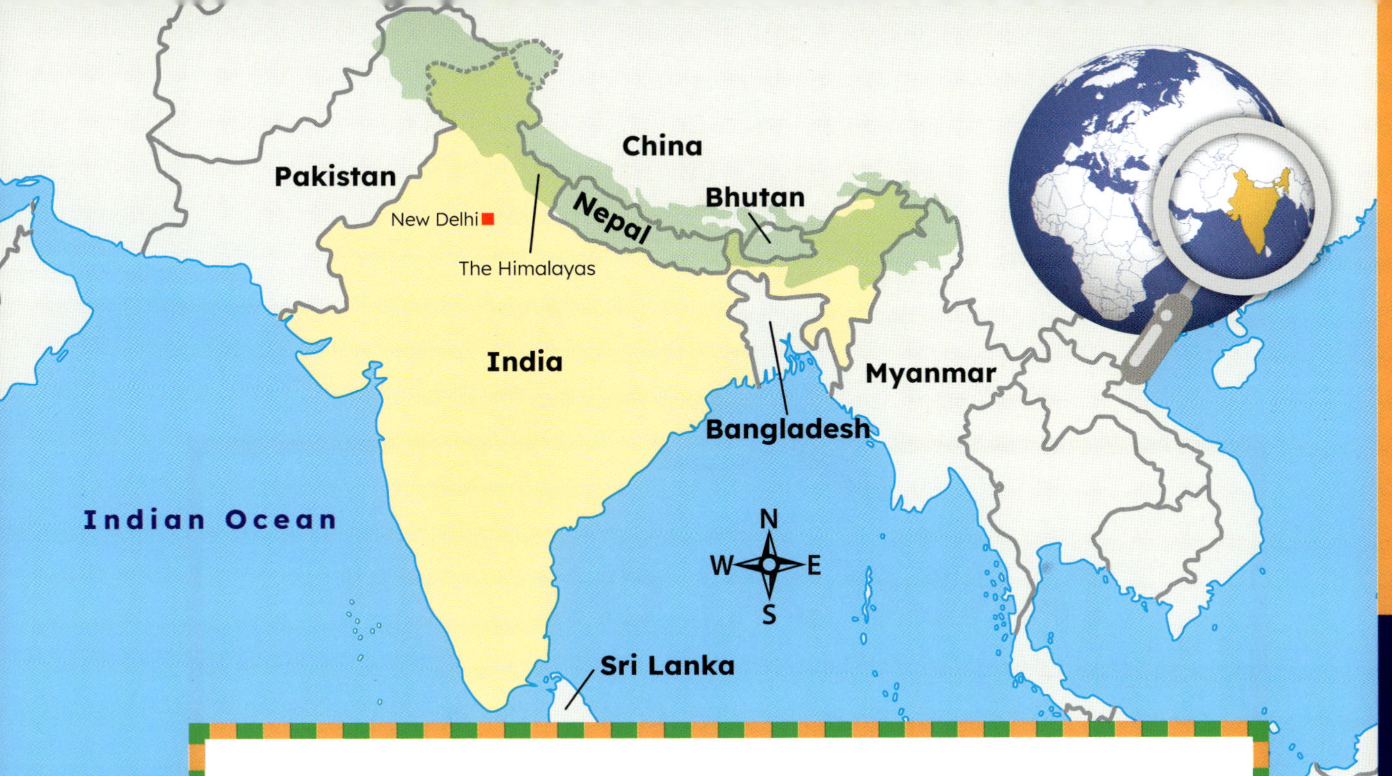

Cows are traditionally viewed as **sacred** in this religion. Because of this, beef is not a common ingredient. Indian cooking uses many different spices. These include saffron, cloves, and turmeric.

Diwali is a Hindu festival of lights. Vendors sell sweet treats during the five days of the festival. One of these is *jalebi* (juh-LAY-bee), a deep-fried spiral. Another is *gulab jamun* (goo-LAHB JAH-moon), deep-fried dough balls served in a sweet syrup.

TANDOORI CHICKEN

Tandoori (tan-DOO-ree) chicken is made in a tandoor oven. This is a big, round clay or metal oven heated with charcoal. Using a tandoor to cook the chicken gives it a smoky flavor. Tandoori chicken is known for its bright-red color.

Tandoori chicken gets its name from the tandoor oven in which it is cooked.

Tandoori chicken's bright-red color comes from the spices in the marinade.

The first step to making tandoori chicken is preparing a yogurt **marinade**. Yogurt, ginger, garlic, ground pepper, and lemon juice are added to a bowl. Ground coriander, **garam masala** powder, cumin powder, red chili powder, and salt are added as well. Everything is whisked together. Then paprika powder and vegetable oil are added. The ingredients are whisked again.

Next, the chicken is prepared. Cooks remove the skin. Then they cut the chicken into quarters. The chicken is added to the marinade. It is important to fully cover the chicken with the marinade. The chicken usually marinates overnight.

Finally, it is time to cook the chicken. The chicken is put onto a large metal rod called a skewer. The skewer is placed inside the tandoor. The chicken is roasted for 15 to 20 minutes. It will be bright red and slightly charred. The yogurt makes the chicken taste tangy. All of the spices make it hot. Tandoori chicken is often served with basmati rice. It is also served with a flatbread called *naan* (NAHN).

FLATBREADS IN INDIAN CUISINE

Flatbreads are often served as a side to Indian dishes. Naan is chewy and made with yogurt. It can be traced back to 1300 AD. Naan is traditionally baked on the walls of a tandoor oven. *Paratha* (pah-RAH-tah) is flaky. It is cooked in a pan. *Roti* (ROH-tee) is thin, like a Mexican tortilla. *Dosa* (DOH-sah) is like a crêpe. It is made with ground lentils or rice.

Naan is often served with tandoori chicken.

SAMOSAS

Samosas (suh-MOH-suhs) are a popular snack. A samosa is dough filled with a mixture of green peas, spices, and potatoes. They sometimes include meat. But they are usually vegetarian. Samosas are triangular.

To make samosas, potatoes are peeled and boiled. Once they are cooked, the potatoes are crumbled. The samosa dough is made with flour, carom seeds, salt, and ghee. Ghee is a **clarified** butter.

Samosas are a tasty snack food.

Samosas are a popular street food in India.

The dough ingredients are mixed until they look like bread crumbs. Water is slowly added into the dough mixture. The dough forms a ball when it is ready. It is then covered with a towel for 20 to 30 minutes.

While the dough rests, cooks prepare the filling. Cumin seeds are heated in a pan with ghee. Ginger and green chilies are added to the pan. More spices come next. These include red chili and cumin powder, salt, garam masala, **chaat masala**, and fennel powder. Green peas and potatoes come next. The ingredients are **sautéed** for a few minutes. Cooks add chopped cilantro to the mixture.

Then the cook works on the dough again. Cooks knead the dough. They separate it into smaller pieces. Each piece is rolled out into a circle. The circle is then cut in half. The straight side of the semicircle is smoothed with water. Then it is folded together and pinched to make a cone. The potato mixture goes inside. The remaining edges are smoothed with water. They are pinched tightly to seal the cone. The samosas are then deep-fried in a pan of oil. These snacks are golden and crispy. They are often served with chutney or other dipping sauces.

Dipping sauces such as chutney are often served with samosas.

WHAT IS CHUTNEY?

Chutney is a savory, sweet, or spicy condiment. Chutney has its roots in India. Two common chutneys are mint and tamarind. Mint chutney is bright green. It has a spicy and refreshing flavor. The dark-brown tamarind chutney is sweet and sour.

MANGO LASSI

Mango *lassi* (luh-SEE) is a refreshing yogurt drink. It is perfect for hot summer days. Lassi tastes sweet. It has a silky-smooth texture. It is traditionally made with *dahi* (DUH-hee) yogurt. This is less sour than other yogurts.

Chilled ingredients are best for lassi. That way, the drink stays cold. First, mangoes are peeled and chopped. Then the chopped mangoes, cardamom powder, sugar, and milk are added to a blender.

Mango lassi is a cool, sweet drink.

With a blender and a few ingredients, anyone can make mango lassi.

The ingredients are blended until smooth. Then the yogurt is added. It is blended just enough to mix.

Finally, the lassi is poured into glasses. Saffron and chopped pistachios can be used as a **garnish**. The drink should taste sweet, fruity, and rich.

WONDER MORE

Wondering about New Information

How much did you know about Indian cuisine before reading this book? What new information did you learn? Write down three new facts you learned from this book. Was the new information surprising? Why or why not?

Wondering How It Matters

Why do you think it is important to learn about foods from different countries? How can learning about and trying new foods affect your life? Are there any foods from India you would like to try?

Wondering Why

Indian food uses many kinds of spices. Why do you think spices are used in recipes? How do different spices change the taste of food? What is your favorite spice?

Ways to Keep Wondering

Indian food is eaten all over the world. After reading this book, what questions do you have about it? What can you do to learn more about Indian food?

MANGO LASSI RECIPE

With an adult's help, try making this mango lassi. Dahi yogurt can be found in Indian supermarkets. Greek yogurt mixed with milk or cream can be used as an alternative.

Ingredients

- 1 ½ cups chopped frozen mangoes
- ½ cup whole milk
- 2 to 3 tablespoons sugar
- ¼ teaspoon cardamom powder
- 1 cup plain dahi yogurt
- Saffron or sliced pistachios (optional)

Steps

1. Add mangoes, milk, sugar, and cardamom powder to a blender. Blend until smooth.
2. Spoon yogurt into the blender. Blend until the yogurt is mixed in. It should be a thick, smooth consistency.
3. Pour the mango lassi into glasses. Garnish with saffron or sliced pistachios if desired.

GLOSSARY

chaat masala (CHOT muh-SAH-lah) Chaat masala is an Indian spice blend that includes mango powder, black salt, and other ingredients. Chaat masala is used to make samosas.

clarified (KLAYR-ih-fyed) Clarified butter is butter that has had all of the milk solids removed. Ghee is a kind of clarified butter.

cuisines (kwih-ZEENZ) Cuisines are styles of cooking. Indian cuisines are enjoyed all over the world.

garam masala (GUH-rum muh-SAH-lah) Garam masala is an Indian spice blend that includes black pepper, cumin, cinnamon, and other ingredients. Garam masala is used in many Indian dishes.

garnish (GAR-nish) A garnish is an ingredient placed on top of a meal for decoration or extra flavor. Pistachios can be used as a garnish for mango lassi.

marinade (MAYR-ih-nayd) A marinade is a sauce in which meat or vegetables are soaked to add flavor and make meat more tender. Yogurt and spices make the marinade for tandoori chicken.

sacred (SAY-krid) When something is sacred, it is considered holy and important to someone's religion or beliefs. Cows are sacred in Hinduism, so Hindus typically do not eat beef.

sautéed (saw-TAYD) When food is sautéed, it is fried in a hot pan with butter or oil. The ingredients of samosa filling are sautéed before being wrapped in the dough.

savory (SAY-vuh-ree) When a food is savory, it tastes salty or spicy. Chutney can be savory or sweet.

staple (STAY-puhl) A staple food is one that people eat almost every day. Rice is a staple of Indian cuisine.

tropical (TRAW-pih-kull) A tropical climate is one where temperatures usually do not dip below freezing. Most of India has a tropical climate.

FIND OUT MORE

In the Library

Doeden, Matt. *Travel to India.* Minneapolis, MN: Lerner Publications, 2022.

Perkins, Chloe, and Tom Woolley. *Living in India.* New York, NY: Simon Spotlight, 2016.

VeLure Roholt, Christine. *Foods of India.* Minneapolis, MN: Bellwether, 2014.

On the Web

Visit our website for links about foods from India:
childsworld.com/links

Note to Parents, Caregivers, Teachers, and Librarians: We routinely verify our Web links to make sure they are safe and active sites. So encourage your readers to check them out!

INDEX